FENG SHUI
A Guide for Home Use

by Karen Ward

Dip F.S., B. Soc. Sc.

Published by
Amberwood Publishing Ltd
Guildford, England

PLANTLIFE

The Natural History Museum, Cromwell Road, London SW7 5BD

Registered Charity No. 328576

Amberwood Publishing supports the Plantlife Charity, Britain's only charity exclusively dedicated to saving wild plants.

ISBN 1-899308-23-7

Cover design by Howland Northover

Illustrations by Morgan Read.

Printed in Great Britain

CONTENTS

Acknowledgements

Thanks to everyone who has helped with this book – especially TB for your input, and Stephen for your suggestions. Also thanks to Jackie for being patient and to UM for being there when needed.

About the Author

Karen Ward's interest in Feng Shui originated from her love of both the natural world and the healing arts. Whilst studying Geography at Bristol University, she also began learning the gentle Chinese exercise T'ai Chi. Since then she has set up several businesses in the natural health field, and has at the same time pursued her T'ai Chi practice. This experience led her to develop the ability to sense subtle energies. Noticing the effects of different environments on her own energy gave Karen an insight into the importance of places in influencing well-being. This took her on to the study of Feng Shui.

Karen set up the Bristol School of Aromatherapy and Reflexology in 1995, and has been involved in the establishment and management of professional training courses, whilst also developing her Feng Shui consultancy. In 1999 she decided to give up her work at the School to concentrate on her growing Feng Shui and Earth Acupuncture services and T'ai Chi teaching. She currently advises on Feng Shui for individual and business clients UK wide, and provides an Earth Acupuncture service. For more information she can be contacted on (01462) 436732. Karen is a member of the Feng Shui Society and Shen Dao Institute.

Author's Note

The art of Feng Shui is becoming increasingly popular in the West as we strive to lead more balanced, less stressful lives. This book has been written for people who have heard of Feng Shui and want to find out more about it. It is an introductory guide, rather than an in-depth study and as such, it will cover common principles and beliefs underlying this fascinating subject.

The guide will also give you practical suggestions on how to change the Feng Shui of your home for the better. Please note – if you think you have a serious Feng Shui problem, it is advisable to seek the help of a professional consultant, just as it is sensible to consult a doctor about health problems.

I hope you enjoy making changes to the Feng Shui in your immediate environment, and that you life becomes more harmonious as a result.

Note to Reader

Foreword

The first approach to any subject is often the most critical. This is particularly so with the ancient Eastern topic of Feng Shui.

As a practitioner and lecturer I am often asked to suggest reading material on the subject, and it is refreshing to be able to recommend a book in its entirety, for its simplicity and plain speaking. The principles are encompassed and explained without prejudicing the reader and without complication. It opens the door for the reader to use their own observations of the environment in a new light and begin to understand and implement Feng Shui to improve this.

This book sets out the ground rules that can be applied in our home environment, which can be agreed and recommended by consultants, lecturers and authorities of every branch or school of Feng Shui, and as such forms an excellent introduction to this subject.

Simon Southall
Director of the Shen Dao Institute of Feng Shui

1 | Feng Shui – power of place

Introduction

The use of Feng Shui is becoming very widespread in the West both by individuals and in businesses. Its popularity is growing as we seek to find a more balanced way of living.

Feng Shui provides us with a way of altering places in order to create a harmonious environment. It is based on the idea of 'chi', an energy force which flows through everything. In this book we're going to consider why the Feng Shui of your home is important, and different methods of improving the chi in your surroundings.

We live within space, and by altering factors in our environment we can improve its Feng Shui. This in turn can dramatically improve our well-being, which influences other aspects of life such as health, prosperity and relationships.

Feng Shui is an ancient practice which developed over 3000 years ago in China. It was used by Emperors, particularly for finding appropriate burial sites for relatives. Through its long history it has evolved, and is now applied to places where we live and work.

'Feng' means wind, 'Shui' means water. These are two forces fundamental in nature. Without water we would have droughts, food would not grow, little would survive, humans would die. Wind is the force which moves water, by transporting vapour in the form of clouds and is also the force of dispersal, moving seeds to new areas, circulating and mixing gases. Without wind (air), there would be no movement in the atmosphere which gives us fresh air to breathe. The interplay of these two forces is fundamental in the physical world. In Feng Shui, concepts of 'wind' and 'water' are used to describe the flow of energy which moves around in the same way that these elements do.

Energy in our environment

Feng Shui is based on the idea of 'chi' – the energy of life, the life force which permeates everything. In Feng Shui the environment is full of chi. This chi moves around and changes, just as the weather does from day to day. The aim of Feng Shui is to harmonise it, so it is beneficial for us. If chi is flowing and positive then our home will feel better and so will we. We are influenced, usually subconsciously, by the places in which we spend most of our time, and this is mainly the home or workplace.

Think about all the different people's homes you have visited. Can you remember one where, on entering, you immediately felt restless, oppressed, or drained without knowing why. It could be that this was caused by poor Feng Shui. Contrast this with the easy, pleasant feelings that can be experienced in living areas where chi is good.

Long term effects of places

We often underestimate how much our home can affect us. One which has poor chi can leave us feeling tired, irritable, or with many other negative feelings. Why should this be? Because we spend so much time there, and whether we are aware of it or not, we constantly pick up the 'vibes' or energy of our environment.

The affect our surroundings have on us is subtle. If you study how you feel in different places you will become more aware of how they affect you. In places with good chi we may experience a range of beneficial feelings. We feel energised, relaxed, positive, calm, and so on. In places with disturbed chi we may feel uneasy, drained, chaotic or irritable.

Over time a home with bad Feng Shui can have an effect on our overall well-being. It's rather like eating a small amount of toxic substance each day. At first we don't notice the effects, our body processes it. After a period of time the substance builds up until we have a toxic overload, and we are then aware of being 'poisoned'. The same concept applies to the energy in our home. If we are constantly absorbing disturbed chi – this can build up to a significant level and cause illness or irrational emotions. It is possible to avoid many of these problems once we become more aware of how our homes actually affect us.

EXERCISE

When you visit different homes, notice how you feel as soon as you walk through the door. Can you sense the 'mood' or 'feel' of a place? How do you feel when you leave compared to when you entered? How does this vary on different visits? Can you pinpoint why? Keep a diary of your discoveries.

In the following chapters we will look at the main principles underlying Feng Shui. Then we'll study chi in more depth – how it flows into buildings, what it likes and dislikes. We'll follow this by considering the Feng Shui of your home with many helpful hints and tips. Finally we'll explore ways to enhance the chi in your home.

But first here's a quiz (overleaf) to help you assess your home's present Feng Shui. Repeat the quiz a few months from now, once you've put the advice in this book into action, to see how your scores compare.

Q U I Z – *how good is your Feng Shui?*

Answer the following questions honestly with a 'yes' or 'no'. Total up scores given next to each of your answers and refer to the end of the quiz. Give your responses with all members of the household in mind to give a fair overview.

	Yes	No
Do you have more than one pile of magazines, post, bills and other things to sort out?	3	1
Do you have healthy plants in your home?	1	2
Do you sleep under a beam?	3	1
Do you find it difficult to get to sleep?	2	1
Once asleep, do you sleep soundly most of the time?	1	4
Generally is your health better when you are away from home?	4	1
Did your life change dramatically for the worse within three months of the last time you moved?	4	1
Do you have windows in all the rooms in your home?	1	3
Do you often feel drained at home?	4	1
Do you regularly experience emotions with no known cause especially when you're at home (such as anger, irritability, grief)?	4	1
Is your hallway filled with clutter, or furniture, or things which stop you moving easily from room to room?	3	1
Do you have arguments in the same specific places in your home?	3	1
Are rubbish bins visible at the front of your house?	2	1
Does the entrance to your home look well-kept and pleasing to you?	1	3
Do you throw out rubbish (from inside the home) regularly rather than wait until bins overflow?	1	3

Q U I Z – how good is your Feng Shui?

	Yes	No
Is your home dusted and cleaned regularly?	1	3
Do all internal doors open and close easily?	1	2
Do you use a microwave?	3	1
Are there any imposing trees, telegraph posts or buildings outside your home?	4	1
Do friends always suggest you go round to their place (rather than come to yours)?	2	1
Do you feel inspired to cook healthy food in your kitchen?	1	4
Are there any accident blackspots in your home?	3	1
Do you have recurring problems with home electrical equipment?	4	1
Do you have persistent problems with home plumbing and drains?	4	1

How did you score?

Under 30 – Your Feng Shui is in near perfect balance and harmony. Stay in tune, keep enhancing your home's chi, and your home life will be the envy of everyone.

31-45 – Your Feng Shui is fairly good and not hindering your life. However, you could overcome minor irritations by enhancing your home's chi more regularly and benefit your home and everyone in it.

46-55 – Your Feng Shui needs some serious attention – your home is not working for you. Take a good look at your surroundings, then put the suggestions in this book into action and see how life improves.

More than 56 – You live in a Feng Shui disaster zone. Consider moving, or consult a Feng Shui expert as soon as possible.

2 | Feng Shui principles

Chi

Chi is the life force, the universal energy (called 'prana' in Indian traditions) which flows through everything that is living.

Chi in humans

The difference between a living and dead person is that the former has chi, the life force. In humans, chi circulates through the body along energy channels known as 'meridians'. Concentrations of chi (acupuncture points) are found along these pathways.

In acupuncture, needles are inserted into these points to rebalance the body's chi. Recent scientific studies have succeeded in measuring electric potential in these areas. A more subtle chi surrounds the body, commonly called the 'aura'.

We replenish our chi from the food we eat and the water we drink. We also take in chi through breathing and from the environment (through our auras). Exercises such as T'ai chi, yoga and meditation can help us to become more aware of our chi.

Chi in homes

In our homes a good energy field is created by chi which flows naturally (beneficial chi). If it is disrupted, this disturbed energy is called 'sha', essentially good chi turned bad. The aim of Feng Shui is to increase beneficial chi, and minimise the negative effects of sha, to create a balanced living environment. Chi in our home is explored in more depth in Chapter 3.

Yin and Yang

Yin and yang are complementary qualities used to describe things. Yin qualities are receptive, dark, inward, stillness, shade; yang qualities are expansive, brightness, outward, movement, light (see table below). For example, midday is more yang, and night is more yin. A dark coloured room is more yin; a light coloured room more yang.

Yin and Yang are not separate. They are complementary opposites. For example, night is only meaningful if you have the idea of daytime. Heavy only has meaning if you can compare it with lightweight. The symbol used for yin and yang shows the connection between these opposite qualities – yin is dark, and intertwined with yang which is light.

YIN	YANG
Below	Above
Shade	Brightness
Dark	Light
Inward	Outward
Day	Night
Cool	Hot
Contracting	Expanding
Passive	Active
Receptive	Creative
Winter	Summer
Earth	Sky
Female	Male

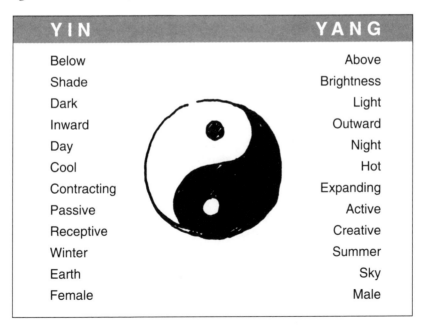

Yin and yang are relative terms, illustrated by looking at the example of how a hill changes over the course of a day. In the morning the eastern side of the hill is more yang as the sun is directly shining on it, compared with the shadowed western side. By mid-afternoon, the sun has moved towards the west, so the eastern side of the hill, now in shadow, is more yin than the western side, now in full sun.

Yin and yang are constantly changing, each containing the seed of the other. For example, daytime is yang and has the seed of night (yin) in it. At dusk yin is growing, yang is declining. At night yin is dominant, but yang is born out of yin, at dawn yang grows, and yin decreases until full day. Thus the balance of these two opposing qualities constantly transforms, one into the other. This is true of everything in life. Hence yin and yang can be used to express the cyclic changes seen in life such as night and day, the seasons, the tides of the sea.

Yin and yang are the basis of much of Chinese philosophy. Concepts such as the Five Elements, the Eight Trigrams, the 64 Hexagrams and I Ching are derived from this elementary idea.

Balance

The idea of balance is central to Feng Shui. Our lives are constantly changing over time – we meet new people, babies are born, people die, we buy new possessions, we come into money, we have financial problems, we enjoy good health, we become ill, we change careers, we have new experiences. Life is not a constant but 'change' is one of the few certain factors in our lives. Many changes occur every day – some have little effect on us, some are quite dramatic.

In Feng Shui, we aim to balance the home to be in harmony with the here and now. What is right at one point may not be appropriate five years later. We also take a holistic approach to life – balance is about achieving harmony of mind, body and spirit, rather than just fixing a problem. Often when our Feng Shui is not in balance this is a reflection of other unfulfilled aspects of life – such as creativity or spirituality.

We also seek to find a balance with nature which provides us with resources of food, water and shelter. We should aim to be guardians of the natural world, rather than seeking to control it. Even in a city, there is a sky above, earth below, and usually water flowing nearby. The more we live in harmony with the forces of nature, the more balanced our life will be.

Interaction of humans and space

In Feng Shui it is considered that different aspects of life such as relationships, career, and wealth are interconnected, each having a possible influence on the other. An example of this would be at the time of a new romantic friendship when old friends are seen less, or altered concentration levels might affect work. During this period one's socialising pattern may alter and regular spending habits change considerably. With careful study it becomes apparent the new relationship has influenced behaviour and caused a chain reaction in lifestyle. Environment is just another state within this pattern with its own energy and in a similar way exerting its own influence.

If the chi in a home is disturbed it can cause a wide range of negative emotions, ranging from irritability, restlessness and feelings of being drained. It is understandable if partners, children or colleagues in the workplace are in turn affected adversely, or that precious "leisure time" is frittered away.

There is a constant interaction between environment and human behaviour, one bearing on the other and leaving an underlying atmosphere. This can be felt in rooms where people have been unhappy or major arguments have happened. It is easy to sense such an atmosphere. Strong emotions of any sort can leave an "imprint" in the form of a "feeling" on the chi of a home.

Interactions between humans and the space they live in can help create the environment. All aspects influencing the other in a constant moving force. It can be positive or negative. If Feng-Shui is good, life will also feel good and the benefits will be felt everyday in many ways.

If it is bad, the negative effects can be minimised by making small improvements that will solve problems and help change direction.

Approaches to Feng Shui

Feng Shui principles are applied in many different ways. Some are extremely complex and beyond the scope of this book. An overview of the main approaches follows.

Form School

Form School concentrates on two main areas – dragons and the Four Animals. Chi moves in the countryside through 'dragon lines' (which are comparable to meridians in the human body – both carry chi). These lines follow the landscape's forms – hills, mountains, valleys. Water dragons are associated with movement of energy along water courses.

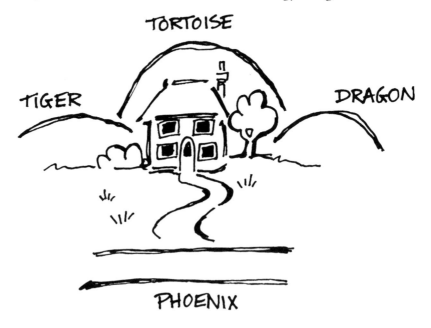

The Four Animals

The Four Animals refer to the black tortoise, green dragon, red phoenix, white tiger. These are symbolic, each representing a different kind of energy. The ideal spot for a home is with a high mountain or building behind (representing tortoise), a significant rise/hill to the right (symbolising dragon), a low hill to east (symbolic of tiger), and flat land to the front (to encourage energy of the phoenix). The concepts of Form School are used as a map which can be adapted for use in any building, or in internal rooms.

Compass School
The Compass School of Feng Shui uses complex methods to assess the energy of a place according to directions and influences on the movement of chi. Traditional Compass methods assess the type of chi according to cardinal directions: north/south/east/west. The Directional Compass method considers directions of chi according to perceptual space.

The Pa Kua or Ba Gua is a tool used in some branches of Compass approach as a symbolic tool (derived from ying/yang theory). The octagonal Ba Gua is used as a map signifying different aspects of life and is overlaid on a diagram of the home, or specific rooms. It is orientated in different ways according to the underlying philosophy of the approach being used. Aspects of life represented by the segments of the Ba Gua are: knowledge, family, wealth, fame, relationships, children, friends, career. These can be improved by using specific enhancements, which vary according to approach.

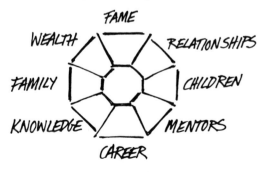

Intuitive / Traditional Approach

This stresses the importance of feeling chi in the environment, aiming to enhance its vibrations to be more harmonious for those who live there. It is often combined with traditional Feng Shui "do's and don'ts", knowledge which has been handed down through generations. It covers placement of beds, effect of beams, position of cookers, and so on. Much of this information is based on common sense, and is used to create a positive environment.

3 | Chi in your home

Surface chi flow in houses

Chi enters a house through the front door, flows through the home and leaves by windows and back doors, drains and toilets. To a lesser extent it also exits through open chimneys. The movement of chi varies from home to home depending on the layout of the building. The easiest way to get a sense of this flow is to imagine coloured smoke being blown in through the front door. You would see the smoke flowing and eddying, weaving its way through your house. Chi movement would be very similar to this.

Underground chi

A more substantial kind of chi is present under the ground. This affects the energy of the home above, and can cause persistent problems for residents if it is unbalanced. Earth Acupuncture is a technique used to release blockages in the flow of this underground energy (consult a specialist if you suspect this is a problem). It is similar to acupuncture for humans.

What good chi likes

Beneficial chi moves in curves, flowing gently like water in a stream or air in a light breeze. Healthy chi flows freely, without obstruction or being too controlled, and likes to form pools (like water pools in a pond). It is also attracted to brightness and is more evident where environments are kept clean.

Disturbances of chi – 'sha'

When chi is not flowing or is forced to flow in straight lines it changes into a disturbed and inbalanced energy called 'sha'. Sha takes many forms but is essentially unhappy chi. In the home environment the most common forms of sha are:

Speed Sha – chi which flows too fast, usually moving in straight lines. This is found in long corridors, or where the front door is directly opposite the back door.

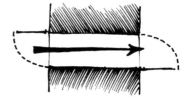

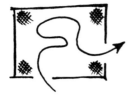

Stagnant Sha – chi which flows too slowly tends to stagnate. For example stagnant sha is often found in corners of rooms, and in basements.

Blocked Sha – where flowing chi is blocked. For example blocked sha is found in areas where clutter or objects obstruct smooth movement of chi.

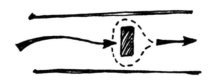

Chaotic Sha – chi which has no obvious direction in which to flow. This type of sha is formed where chi bounces off smooth shiny surfaces like a pinball. It is also found where there is a lot of movement in different directions. For example entrances to stairwells in big blocks of flats often have this type of sha. Mains electrical equipment can also create chaotic sha.

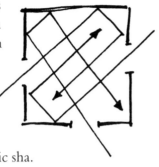

Cutting Sha – often called 'poison arrows' or 'secret arrows'. Where chi flows off sharp edges it forms straight-line energy. It is a very focused type of sha. For example indoors sharp-edged furniture and externally, corners of nearby buildings pointing towards one's home can cause cutting sha.

Type of sha	How it makes us feel
Speed Sha	Rushed, unable to focus.
Stagnant Sha	Lethargic, dull, drained.
Blocked Sha	Stuck, irritable, unable to move on.
Chaotic Sha	Unsettled, indecisive, unfocused, fidgety.
Cutting Sha	Uneasy, restless, angry. Over a long period of time threatened or ill.

To live in greater harmony with our environment we need to reduce the effect of sha, and enhance the chi in our homes. The next two chapters will explain how to do this in greater detail.

4 | Feng Shui in your home

In this chapter we will look at the Feng Shui of your home in more depth, starting outside and working in.

Influences from outside

As the main chi entering your home comes from outside, it is important to take a good look at its exterior. What buildings or landscape face your front door? If you live opposite a prison, the chi may pick up a vibration of anger and resentment – bringing sha rather than beneficial chi into your home. Place an object such as a fence, statue or shrub in the line of the offending external influence and your front door to minimise its impact.

If your house is on a busy road it may be troubled by speed sha. Hang a lead-faceted crystal in your front window to disperse its effect.

Other external structures which impose on the house (as seen from the windows) can affect the internal chi of your home. To intercept dominating influences such as telegraph poles, blocks of flats and other imposing buildings, screen them from sight with net/muslin curtains or put plants on the window-sill to break up the view. If the imposing structure is very near it may be preferable to fit frosted or stained glass in the windows

Main entrance

A positive and welcoming entrance can have a considerable effect on the quality of chi entering your home. The entrance should be tidy and well-kept. Next time you return home, stop at your main entrance and consider what you like and dislike about it.

Ideally you should have a boundary area between the front door and the road (path or lane), with a gate and a fence (wall or hedge) to denote a clear boundary between your territory and public space. Curved pathways to the front door are preferable. If you have a straight path, use planted shrubs or potted plants to create a curved effect and encourage beneficial chi.

The front door is the way in to your world, so it should be welcoming to you. If it makes you feel uninspired or depressed, it may need some attention. Spruce up old and flaking paintwork, tidy up generally, and place flowering plants or hanging baskets to enhance the chi. Rubbish bins and junk should be removed as they will cause blocked sha. Screen bins from view behind a hedge or a small fence. The main door should be solid and sturdy, to ensure adequate separation between inside and out. If you have a choice of main entrances, use one which enters into a hallway, rather than a door which leads directly into a room.

Hallways and staircases

A hallway's function is to separate the outside of the home from internal rooms. As it is the first part of the home you enter, it is good to have a positive picture just inside, in your line of vision. Hallways

23

are also passageways for the flow of chi from outside and should be kept free of clutter. Avoid piling up magazines, boxes, and so on, as this obstructs the flow of chi. Long hallways should be broken up using pictures, wall-hangings, or small tables.

Where the front door opens into a long straight hallway speed sha can be a problem. Putting up a wind-chime or hanging plant will slow down the flow of energy.

Staircases directly opposite the front door are not ideal as energy will rush upstairs. To prevent this position a hanging wind-chime or plant in the hallway. If there is no hallway it is better to use a curtain across the bottom of the stairs instead.

Ceilings and walls

Sloping ceilings found in top floors create a particular Feng Shui problem. If the ceiling slopes lower than shoulder height, the chi gets seriously compressed. Sitting or living in such areas can make us feel constricted or cause frequent headaches or neckaches. Use  areas adjacent to sloping ceilings for low seating or for furniture. Uplighting can help create a sense of space.

Beams are similar to sloping ceilings as they cause compression of chi in the space directly below. Avoid sitting with your head directly under a beam. Traditional Feng Shui advice is to hang two bamboo flutes on the beam, each at a 45 degree angle to it, and pointing towards each other.

Alternatively you can use ornamental hangings, woven items or dried bunches of flowers on the beam. End supports are also effective at reducing the chi compression effect of beams.

Walls which form a 90 degree angle can cause cutting sha so it is advisable to avoid sitting or sleeping in the direct line of such a sharp edge.

Cover very sharp edges with rounded plaster or wood mouldings available from DIY shops. Alternatively hang a scarf or place a plant to obscure most of the edge as an effective means of overcoming the sha.

Kitchens

Kitchens are important because they represent the heart of the home, where we nourish ourselves with food to replenish our human chi.

Is your kitchen inviting – a place where you can be creative in preparing food? Use pictures in the kitchen which symbolise health and well-being.

The position of the cooker is important – ideally it should be positioned where you can see the door when you are cooking. If not, place a small mirror near the cooker to reflect it.

Microwaves destroy chi. Kirlian photos comparing food cooked traditionally and by microwave show that microwaved food loses all its life energy so try to minimise their use.

Avoid a build-up of rubbish in the kitchen — empty bins and clean up spills, dirt and clutter regularly. This should be a yang area of the house, so use bright colours and good lighting.

S U M M A R Y

- Position cookers so you can see the kitchen door when cooking.
- Throw out rubbish regularly.
- Keep kitchen clean and clutter-free.
- Put up pictures symbolic of health and well-being.

Living rooms

The function of a living room varies. For some people it is predominantly a place to relax and enjoy free time. Others may use it mostly for socialising.

Either way a living room benefits from having a focal point. Unless we create one, the television automatically becomes the centre of attention. Try moving your furniture around another focus such as a fireplace, or a central coffee table with a vase of fresh flowers on it.

Sitting with your back to the door is not the best way to relax. Ideally place chairs so none put you in this position. Use a screen or cupboard to obscure the television or cover it with a silk scarf when not in use.

SUMMARY

- Position seating around a pleasant focus point.
- Avoid sitting with your back to the door.
- Avoid too many contrasting patterns.
- Use plants in corners to enhance chi.
- Screen off televisions and computers when not in use.

Bedrooms

We spend approximately one-third of our life asleep, usually in the bedroom. We probably spend more time here than anywhere else. Good quality sleep is vital to recharge us, and for our general health. So sleeping in a beneficial place is important, or we will soon feel the consequences.

When we are asleep our subconscious needs to feel secure so placement of the bed is important. The bedroom is also a sanctuary from the world and should be a peaceful place. Bedrooms should not be multipurpose rooms used as studies, lounges and so on. This is too yang. They should be reserved for sleep and intimate relationships.

Bed position – try not to place the bed with the foot directly facing the bedroom door.

Avoid placing the head of the bed against a window. When sleeping, your head should be protected by a solid wall. Orientate the bed so that you are able to see the bedroom door (but not directly facing out).

Mirrors should not be positioned directly opposite the end of the bed. Move them to another part of the room, or cover with a scarf when not in use. If your sleep is often disturbed it may help to cover all mirrors at night.

Minimise the use of television in the bedroom as it creates chaotic sha, and cover the screen with a cloth at night. Sleeping under beams or overhanging cupboards should be avoided as they exert a compressing effect. Placing the bed in direct line of wall edges which are sending out cutting sha is also inadvisable (see Walls and Ceilings).

Avoid having strong electromagnetic fields near the bed, as they may affect your health. Clock radios should be placed at least 1m (3ft) from your head, and electric blankets should be unplugged before you go to sleep.

SUMMARY

- Position head of bed against a solid wall.
- Avoid bed position where your feet point directly out of the bedroom door when sleeping.
- Minimise use of televisions, and cover screen with a cloth at night.
- Do not place mirrors directly facing foot of bed (or cover at night with a scarf or cloth).
- Avoid equipment which produces electromagnetic fields.
- Avoid sleeping under beams.
- Check for edges causing cutting sha near the bed.
- Ensure bedroom has sufficient privacy.

Bathroom and toilets

Bathrooms and toilets are the waste removal system of the home in terms of energy. Ideally they should be next to an external wall, rather than in the centre. A traditional Chinese Feng Shui belief is that money is associated with water, hence bathrooms and toilets, which are the main drainage points, can cause wealth to flow out of the home. In order to minimise this, keep the door to the toilet and bathroom closed when not in use (some people prefer to keep the toilet lid down in preference). This is especially important when the toilet is positioned directly opposite the front door. En suite bathrooms pose Feng Shui problems. Screen off the door if possible, or keep the door closed when not in use. En suites are often internal windowless rooms, so we instinctively leave doors open to avoid build-up of stagnant chi, but this creates the risk of beneficial chi draining from the home.

SUMMARY

- Keep bathroom and toilet doors closed.
- Screen off en suite bathrooms.
- Avoid clutter which stops efficient removal of waste.
- If possible, toilets should not be opposite the front door.

5 | Enhancing chi in your home

There are many different ways to enhance the chi in your home to improve your well-being.

Cleaning

Make a point of cleaning regularly as beneficial chi is degraded by dirt and dust. Also avoid accumulating waste – throw out rubbish before it builds up. We know how good we feel after a spring clean – this is because we get rid of dust and clutter and the chi of our home is enhanced, make a point of doing this at least once a year.

Clutter

Getting rid of clutter is the most immediate way to ensure that positive chi flows more smoothly. Often we hoard things just because they might come in useful sometime, which causes blockages in our life.

Dispensing with what you no longer need will release you and make space for new things to flow into your life. Check the following and get rid of anything no longer required: those piles on tables and floors; in drawers and wardrobes; on top and down the sides of cupboards; under the bed; in the garage, the attic and the understairs cupboard; and anywhere else clutter can lurk.

Emotional clutter – mementos kept for every occasion to remind us of the past – does more than this by keeping us tied to it, unable to live fully in the present and preventing us from moving on. Keep just a few valued things, rather than a houseful.

Organising your home also reduces the amount of clutter created from not having designated storage places. A laundry basket creates a home for dirty washing. A shoe rack makes space for storing shoes. It's amazing how much more smoothly your life flows when you know where to find everything.

Light

Daylight – Good lighting keeps chi 'bright', and daylight is especially important. Have you ever been in a room that never sees the light of day, where the curtains are always closed, or where there is no window? It will seem lifeless unless there is some other form of chi enhancement. Let light into your home by drawing curtains in the daytime, and keep windows clean so good quality light can enter.

Artificial light – Use good artificial lighting for dark areas and inner hallways. Spotlights or uplighters in the right place can give a spacious feel to such areas of your home, and almost always have a better effect than a central light. Avoid fluorescent strip lights as they cause chaotic sha.

Firelight – Open fires are a good way to purify the atmosphere and shift chi that is becoming stagnant. Candles help to calm down chaotic sha. Use them in your home as an addition to artificial lighting in the evening, or when you want the atmosphere to become more peaceful.

Mirrors

Use mirrors to reflect light to make areas look more spacious. They also help to redirect energy within the home, such as on landings or in hallways. As a general rule mirrors should not be placed directly facing a window or opposite the front door.

Colours

Colours are a reflection of certain light vibrations. Choose colours for decoration which you particularly like. Be experimental – a complete change of colour can have a dramatic positive effect. If you want to raise the chi use brighter colours. Dark tones are very yin, and should not be used too much.

There are different approaches to choosing colour in Feng Shui, according to Five Elements, ba gua or association preferences. As a general rule choose colours according to the way you want a particular room to feel – bright colours for more active rooms, paler colours for more restful areas. Blues and purples tend to cool and calm; reds, oranges, pinks and yellows stimulate and warm; greens balance and soothe.

Water

Flowing water helps chi to circulate. It decreases stagnant and blocked sha. A water feature or fish tank can help to energise areas and create beneficial chi, and can also encourage the flow of wealth. Water features are containers where the water is pumped round to create flowing water, like a mini stream. They are available from many garden centres and DIY stores.

Sound

We're increasingly bombarded with noise from many sources such as traffic, electric garden tools, barking dogs and car alarms. Melodious music can reduce its impact. Choose some which you really like and which suits how you feel at the time. A good indicator of music beneficial to the chi of your home is if you feel calm but energised after listening to it. Wind chimes, bells and drums can also enliven chi which is stagnant or blocked. However, do remember to respect your neighbours' need for peace and quiet at times.

Natural objects

Natural materials are more closely linked to nature, and generally have a more positive influence on chi than man-made. Choose fabrics and materials for soft furnishings made of cotton, linen, wool, silk, rather than synthetics.

For ornaments you can use objects that come directly from nature such as pebbles, wood and shells, and seasonal items from your local environment like horse chestnuts and pine cones.

Crystals can also be used but take care. Crystals can magnify chi, but they may magnify underground sha if placed inappropriately. If you feel a crystal is in the wrong place, trust your intuition and move it.

Plants and flowers

Plants and flowers have a vibrancy of chi which is difficult to obtain from other sources.

Use them to enhance areas in your home such as corners where chi may stagnate. Plants can also be placed in front of, or trailed over, sharp wall edges to reduce cutting sha. Flowers can be used as focal points, but remember to replace them when they start to look jaded.

Symbolic objects and pictures

Our unconscious mind takes in everything around us, even though our conscious mind can only be aware of a limited number of things at any one time. Hence the objects and pictures we put in our environment can have a subtle effects on us of which we are unaware. Choose some which are meaningful to you, and which make you feel inspired, positive or content. Images and objects which leave you feeling heavy, down, or dull should be avoided. Use uplifting pictures where you want to encourage chi to flow, such as in corridors and stairways.

You can use symbolism to influence your subconscious for specific purposes, as it is aware of much more than the conscious mind. If you are seeking romance, use images or objects with pairs in them, such as two swans, a happy couple, two trees and so on. Likewise if you are seeking to improve your health use images which are symbolic of health and vibrancy — such as a picture of a radiant sun, or a beautiful flower, or a photo of yourself when you were in good health.

Simple patterns and soft shapes

Chi gets confused and becomes chaotic if there are too many contrasting patterns. Avoid using too many designs together (in wallpaper, carpets, upholstery, curtains). Cutting sha may be a problem in rooms filled with many pieces of angular furniture, so use round edges and soft shapes to enhance chi where possible.

Positive mental state

In a chi filled world, thoughts have an energy. The kind of thoughts and emotions we have affect chi. They become imprinted on the chi in our environment, often turning it to sha when disharmonious. Have you ever entered a room with an uncomfortable atmosphere, later finding that someone was very unhappy or very angry? Our emotions and thoughts affect the chi. Clearing the air with someone, can literally mean just that. Positive thoughts and meditation can enhance and harmonise the chi.

Aroma

Aroma has a powerful affect on the chi in our environment. You can use aromatic plants in entrances and in window-boxes to create a sweet-smelling immune boost to the chi of your home.

Natural essential oils of lavender, juniper, rosemary and lemon can be diluted in water and used in a plant sprayer to clear stagnant chi from rooms effectively.

Use a fragrancer to vaporise essential oils to create a lovely aromatic atmosphere in living-rooms. Try different mixes of essential oils to suit your preferences.

6 | Changing with Feng Shui

This book has given you an introduction to the main ideas behind Feng Shui. It has also shown you how places can have a real affect on us, especially our home. We live in a world of unseen energy – chi. By minimising sha and enhancing beneficial chi in our homes we can lead more harmonious lives. Our homes can then contribute to our well-being, rather than being a negative influence on us.

It is important to remember how we interact with our environment. By making changes to your Feng Shui you are starting to interact more consciously with the chi in your home. This in turn can lead to a greater awareness of chi in life in general. So you may start to notice how you are affected by particular places, people, things. By becoming more aware you will start to be more conscious of how you also affect other people, places and things. This is the most fascinating aspect of Feng Shui, as it can open up a whole new world to us. We start to see how we are part of the living universe, and view the world in a more dynamic way.

You may want to find out more by reading other books, take up a yoga or t'ai chi class to help you become more aware of chi, or have a Feng Shui consultation for your home which can be beneficial if you are experiencing repeated problems.

The underlying philosophy of Feng Shui encourages more balance in our homes, and it is also encourages us to take a more holistic approach to life. Once we start to live in harmony with the flow of chi we feel more at ease and content within. We regain a sense of connection to the world we are part of. Enjoy making changes to your Feng Shui!

OTHER BOOKS FROM AMBERWOOD PUBLISHING ARE:

Aromatherapy Lexicon – The Essential Reference by Geoff Lyth and Sue Charles is a colourful, fun way to learn about Aromatherapy. £4.99.

Aromatherapy – The Baby Book by Marion Del Gaudio Mak. An easy to follow guide to massage for the infant or child. £3.99

Aromatherapy – Simply For You by Marion Del Gaudio Mak. A clear, simple and comprehensive guide to Aromatherapy for beginners. £2.99.

Aromatherapy – A Guide for Home Use by Christine Westwood. All you need to know about essential oils and using them. £1.99.

Aromatherapy – for Stress Management by Christine Westwood. Covering the use of essential oils for everyday stress-related problems. £3.50.

Aromatherapy – For Healthy Legs and Feet by Christine Westwood. A guide to the use of essential oils for the treatment of legs and feet. £2.99.

Aromatherapy – The Pregnancy Book by Jennie Supper RM RN MGCP. Jennie Supper, a State Registered Nurse and Midwife explains the use of Aromatherapy during pregnancy and the common conditions which may be treated safely. £5.99

Aromatherapy – A Nurses Guide by Ann Percival SRN. The ultimate, safe, lay guide to the natural benefits of Aromatherapy. Including recipes and massage techniques for many medical conditions and a quick reference chart. £2.99.

Aromatherapy – A Nurses Guide for Women by Ann Percival SRN. Concentrates on women's health for all ages. Including sections on PMT, menopause, infertility, cellulite. £2.99.

Aromatherapy – Essential Oils in Colour by Rosemary Caddy Bsc Hons, ARCS MISP is a unique book depicting the chemistry of essential oils. £9.99.

Aroma Science – The Chemistry & Bioactivity of Essential Oils by Dr Maria Lis-Balchin. With a comprehensive list of the Oils and scientific analysis. Includes sections on the sense of smell and the history of Aromatherapy. £5.99.

Woman Medicine – Vitex Agnus Castus by Simon Mills MA, FNIMH. The story of the herb that has been used for centuries in the treatment of women's problems. £2.99.

Plant Medicine – A Guide for Home Use (New Edition) by Charlotte Mitchell MNIMH. A guide to home use giving an insight into the wonderful healing qualities of plants. £2.99.

Ancient Medicine – Ginkgo Biloba (New Edition) by Dr Desmond Corrigan BSc(Pharms), MA, Phd, FLS, FPSI. Improved memory, circulation and concentration are associated with Ginkgo and explained in this book. £2.99.

Indian Medicine – The Immune System by Dr Desmond Corrigan BSc(Pharms), MA, Phd, FLS, FPSI. An intriguing account of the history of the plant called Echinacea and its power to influence the immune system. £2.99.

Herbal Medicine for Sleep & Relaxation by Dr Desmond Corrigan BSc(Pharms), MA, PhD, FLS, FPSI. A guide to the natural sedatives as an alternative to orthodox drug therapies, drawing on the latest medical research, presented in an easy reference format. £2.99.

Herbal First Aid by Andrew Chevallier BA, MNIMH. A beautifully clear reference book of natural remedies and general first aid in the home. £2.99.

Natural Taste – Herbal Teas, A Guide for Home Use by Andrew Chevallier BA, MNIMH. Contains a comprehensive compendium of Herbal Teas gives information on how to make it, its benefits, history and folklore. £3.50.

Garlic– How Garlic Protects Your Heart by Prof E. Ernst MD, PhD. Used as a medicine for over 4500 years, this book examines the latest scientific evidence supporting Garlic's effect in reducing cardiovascular disease, the Western World's number one killer. £3.99.

Phytotherapy – Fifty Vital Herbs by Andrew Chevallier, the most popular medicinal herbs with uses and advice written by an expert. £6.99

Insomnia – Doctor I Can't Sleep by Dr Adrian Williams FRCP. Written by one of the world's leading sleep experts, Dr Williams explains the phenomenon of sleep and sleeping disorders and gives advice on treatment. With 25% of the adult population reporting difficulties sleeping – this book will be essential reading for many. £2.99.

Eyecare Eyewear – For Better Vision by Mark Rossi Bsc, MBCO. A complete guide to eyecare and eyewear including an assessment of the types of spectacles and contact lenses available and the latest corrective surgical procedures. £3.99.

Arthritis and Rheumatism by Dr John Cosh FRCP, MD. Covers all forms of Arthritis, its effects and the treatments available. £4.95.

All You Ever Wanted To Know About Vitamins by Dr Leonard Mervyn. The ultimate book on nutrition. £6.99.